Sun
in
Days

Sun
in
Days

POEMS

MEGHAN O'ROURKE

W. W. NORTON & COMPANY

Independent Publishers Since 1923

New York | London

For information about permission to reproduce selections from this book, write to
Permissions, W. W. Norton & Company, Inc., 500 Fifth Avenue, New York, NY 10110

For information about special discounts for bulk purchases, please contact
W. W. Norton Special Sales at specialsales@wwnorton.com or 800-233-4830

Manufacturing by Berryville Graphics
Book design by Chris Welch
Production manager: Lauren Abbate

Library of Congress Cataloging-in-Publication Data

Names: O'Rourke, Meghan, author.
Title: Sun in days : poems / Meghan O'Rourke.
Description: First edition. | New York : W. W. Norton & Company, [2017]
Identifiers: LCCN 2017026049 | ISBN 9780393608755 (hardcover)
Classification: LCC PS3615.R586 A6 2017 | DDC 811/.6—dc23
LC record available at https://lccn.loc.gov/2017026049

W. W. Norton & Company, Inc., 500 Fifth Avenue, New York, N.Y. 10110
www.wwnorton.com
W. W. Norton & Company Ltd., 15 Carlisle Street, London W1D 3BS

1 2 3 4 5 6 7 8 9 0

FOR JIM

CONTENTS

II

III

Sun
in
Days

Unforced Error

Once: those long wet Vermont summers.
No money, nothing to do but read books, swim
in the river with men in their jean shorts,
then play bingo outside the church, celebrating when we won.
Nothing seemed real to me and it was all very alive.
It took that long to learn how wrong I was—
over the rim of the horizon the sun burns.
Heidegger: "Every man is born as many men
and dies as a single one."
The bones in us still marrowful.
The moon up there, too, an arctic sorrow.
I'm sorry, another Scotch? Some nuts?
I used to think pressing forward was the point of life,
endlessly forward, the snow falling, gaudily falling.
I made a mistake. Now I have a will. It says when I die
let me live. A white shirt, bare legs, bones beneath.
Numbers on a board. A life can be a lucky streak,
or a dry spell, or a happenstance.
Yellow raspberries in July sun, bitter plums, curtains in wind.

I

Self-Portrait as Myself

And now I, Meghan, have grown tired, have come
to the limits of my aesthetic fidelity. It is nearly summer,
and summer seems shorter to me
and winter longer and longer, as if life with
its inevitable accumulation of griefs
shifts time the way the myth said: casting a layer
of snow over all our losses. I want a daughter, but
the daughter I'll never have I can't imagine
more than I already have. I'd like to say,
these are the stories my mother read me,
and she is gone, and six decades
pass fast, so much faster than the mind absorbs
all the distorted love it feels for the world,
all the knowledge it accrues and wants to continue
to accrue, and in not being able to imagine her—
Stop. Stop here, and feel the light and the heat through
the window by my desk and remember the fields
I've stood in, the prickling of time at my leg,
the propeller planes hymning past, the daughter I lost
by not making her—the RNA, the tethered alleles,
the whorls of her fingers like the twisting
clouds above, the high and possible
voice I'll never hear except within my secret ears.

Sun in Days

1.

I tried to live that way for a while, among
the trees, the green breeze,
chewing Bubblicious by the edge of the pool
The book open on my chest, a towel
at my back the diving board *thwok*ing,
and leaving never arrived   Cut it out
my mother said   my brother
clowning around with a water gun   *Cut it out.*
The planes arrowed into silence, fourteen,
fifteen, sixteen, always coming
home from summer   over the bridge to Brooklyn.
The father stabbed on Orange Street,
the Betamax in the trash,
the Sasha doll the dog chewed up, hollow
plastic arms gaping. Powdered pink lemonade,
tonguing the sweet grains   liquid-thick.
I could stand in that self for years
wondering is it better to
anticipate than to age   Imagining
children with three different men,
a great flood that would destroy
your possessions   and free you to wander.

Bathing suits and apples and suntan oil
and a mother bending over you
shadow of her face on yours. It's gone,
that way, the breeze, the permanent pool.
A father saying "ghost" and the sheets
slipping off the oak tree's bough.
When I wake, leaves
in the water. You could say green
forever and not be lying.

2.

The pond near the house in Maine
where we lived for one year
to "get away" from the city   the pond
where the skaters   on Saturdays came,
red scarves   through white snow,
voices drawing near and   pulling
away, trees against the clouds. Living
off the land for a while. Too hard
in the end my father said. What did he say?
Forget it   you weren't listening   He wore
fishing overalls most days and smelled of guts.
Our shouts slipping, the garbage cans
edging the white scar pond,
so many days like secrets about to be
divulged . . .   White snow;
to stink of fish guts but   to be trying
to live: the pond near the house
and the sound of voices   drawing near.

As you aged you got distracted, indebted.
In the hospital around my mother
the machines   beeped,
the long leads of the heart monitor,

drooping parabolas.

It's not worth dying for   she said. What

was it she meant? Swollen shells, the desiccated brown

seedpods we used to pinch onto our noses

and skate about   putting on airs.

Then the books opened

their pages and with our red woolen

scarves flying   and the Freezy Freakies'

once-invisible hearts reddening

into the cold we disappeared.

Evian bottles skitter against the chain-link fence.

It's gone   that way   the green

planes arrowing into silence   gum wrappers

slipping to the ground.

O wild West wind   be thou our friend

and blow away the trash.

Salvage us from   the heap of our making and

Cut it out my mother said   Stop worrying

about the future, it doesn't

belong to us and we don't belong to it.

3.

The surface more slippery, slick
and white the ice. I stand at the pond's edge
gather the information   darkening there
hello algae   hello fish pond
my mind in the depths   going.
On the beach I dig, tunnel
to the hands of the woman who stitched
this red shirt   digging all the way to China.
It got so easy to   get used to it,
the orchestration of meaning
against the night, life
a tower you could climb on
not a junk heap   pale picture books
yellowing on the shelves rusting
steel mills on the edge of town. It gets
so   I close my eyes
and walk along the hospital hall.
The iris quivering in the March light,
a nurse taking my mother's pulse
not paid enough to help us
as we wished to be helped. And your hope
left behind   turning the pages of magazines,
the models in Prada. As a girl

it was a quest, to feel exploded every second,
Pudding Pops   and Vietnam vets
standing on the corner shaking their Styrofoam
cups.   Holding her
cup my mother stands, petting the dog,
it's 1982   the sun tunneling in   she drinks her coffee
Cut it out or   Forget it or   Hello.
Look, I've made a telephone for us.
Put that cup to your ear, and I'll put it to mine,
and listen   I just need to find
one of those Styrofoam cups
and what about you   where did you
go what kind of night is it there
electric synthetic blackened or burnt.

4.

At night the dead come to you
distorted and bright, like an old print on a light box—
still   happening in a time we can't touch.
The hockey game on the blue
TV glowing and slowing   I come home
to a man slumped on the couch not-quite-saying
hello   all the gone ones there
the slap of skates   all gone
and the commentator it's going on forever
the blade moving along rink
says What a slap shot what a shot.
You make a life, it is made of days and
days, ordinary and subvocal, not busy
becoming what they could be,   dark furlings of
tiny church feelings   mysterious, I mean,
and intricate like that stain-windowed light—

intricate and mysterious   I come home.

We hung out on the Promenade
after school the boys smoking
the security systems in the Center blinking   a disco
party blue red / blue red the East River

below scraped sky   cornices and clouds
we could hear the cars roaring across it
taste the chemical air of the father's offices
where we picked them up
for the long weekend in the Catskills
the hum-gray computers, the IBM Selectrics, eleven, twelve,
thirteen, riding the graffiti'd subways,
flirting, the boys   grabbing us calling   hey hey
snapping our bras and   shame.
At night the bomb   mushrooming
over the Statue of Liberty, white
blinding everywhere.   Oh, my mother said, don't worry
just a dream   just a dream
Everyone is scared of Russia
she laughed   We used to
have to hide under our desks!

Forget it   you weren't listening   I was trying
to tell you something
the maples bare your mother a teenager
Come on the leaves are   sliding past the window
riding a horse into her future
into the river where the Catholic kids sailed ice boats
their uncles wiring cash home to Ireland.
The future isn't here yet, it's always

arriving   but I'm holding you,
walking the Promenade, thirty-six, thirty-seven,
the ferry crossing the river again.

5.

And for a while   rain on the dirt road
and the pastured gray horse   holding Chex Mix
up to its fuzzed mouth   pockets of time
all summer   eating ghosts in the arcade
Pac-Man alive quarter after quarter
I keep trying—Cut it out   she said and
Forget it   I was trying to tell you
my father cooking fish in the kitchen
licking his thumb   to turn the page.

In the meantime you try
not to go into a kind of exile—
Oh, you read too many books, says my friend John.
Turn on the TV. And the small voices
of children   enter the room, they sound
so narrow and light and possible. But
don't you think   we're always making the same
standing at the car rental
kind of mistake we began by making
at the last minute, rushing to call
our parents before setting off
for vacation.   It's warmer
this August than it has been for decades.

Still the sun bathing us isn't preposterous
or cold   Grace: imagine it

and all the afterworld fathers sleeping
with their hair perfectly   combed
faces mortician-clean
unlike the ones they wore.
In the motel Reagan on TV   his hair
in that parted wave   the milk prices up,
my mother says, inflation   her father's
shipping job gone, the money gone.   Key Food
on Montague, the linoleum tiles dirty and cracked,
the dairy case goose-pimpling my skin.
Those tiles are still there.
She is dead now   and so is he.
I know it seems bare to say it
bare to   bare linoleum tiles.

You who come after me
I will be underfoot but
Oh, come off it, start again. We all live
amid surfaces and   and I
wish I had the   Start over   Come on thou

Step into the street amidst
the lightly turning trash,
your hair lifting in the wind   Remember
I have thought of you
the lines of our skates converging
in a future etc., etc., the past
the repository of what can be salvaged, grace
watering the basil
on the windowsill, until
the day comes of   looking back at it all,
like a projectionist at a movie
slipping through the reel, the stripped sound of time—

I tried to live that way for a while
chewing Bubblicious and   spitting it out
Only forget it you   were
if I could hear your voice   again   I could pretend
Rise and shine she called in the morning
Rise and shine   leaves in the water   intricate and personal

the dying Dutch elms the cool blue
pockets of time   gum wrappers underfoot
Sun-In bleaching our hair
the faces they wore   arcade ghosts dying
and lilacs by the door in Maine
where she leaned   close   said Smell
the planes buzzed   a purple light fingers
sticky   if I could only hear it
again   you could say forever   the fisherman
the empty mills   the veterans on the corner
tonguing the sweet grains
you could say forever   and not be lying

Dread

My keys jingling beside the honeysuckle
as we walk home from dinner,
our iPhones glittering with emails

calling us to the things of the world.
The moon wired to the sky
by all the coffee you drank.
Another day, another year.

On our faces, the children we're becoming,
those orphans—

Mnemonic

I look up, it's
September and the tree
in the backyard's
fading, soon enough
it'll be winter,
embered, crisp-curled
leaves matrixed
on the sidewalk,
a Photoshopped
etching. I can't tell
the difference anymore. What
have I done with this year of living?
I fretted & fanged,
was a kind of
slang of myself.
Used to know how to live,
now need a mnemonic,
or glass-bottom
boat tour, including
snorkels & a printed
index (angelfish, shark,
love-of-your-life,
home, catastrophe, grave).
Or an apparatus
for funneling the moon's

milk-light down
on one's skin.
I see you're really me,
lifelike but not alive,
an animal in a diorama.
Wake up, you! Bursting
from the painted hawthorn,
unhurtable, unrealized,
that marvelous
thing you never
imagined has arrived.

Addict Galerie

Outside my Paris sublet
the addict paces, flicking
her dentures in and out
of her pink mouth, like
a rose which is not a rose,
and a new rocking horse
stands in the window
of the neighbors I watch.
Mother, father, child,
a son about two or so
with blond flaking hair.
Often they stand
at the corner window
as if at the prow of a ship
and gaze down Vieille du Temple,
talking aimlessly. I want
this, won't have it.
Something about the way their life looks
from afar, yellow-lamped and
bound by tea and snacks and rocking horses,
the father always working late at his desk.
I thought my body
would work forever,
like a rocking horse,
a Ferris wheel, or grass

returning. Now I carry myself
as a coffin, the sharp corner
digging into my collarbone,
hands sweating
and burning, neck spasming,
a blister at the life line.
I'll never get it to the car.

The Night Where You No Longer Live

Was it like lifting a veil
And was the grass treacherous, the green grass

Did you think of your own mother

Was it like a virus
Did the software flicker

And was this the beginning
Was it like that

Was there gas station food

                and was it a long trip

And is there sun there
       or drones
       or punishment
       or growth

Was it a blackout

       And did you still create me
       And what was I like on the first day of my life

Were we two from the start
And was our time an entrance
or an ending

Did we stand in the heated room
Did we look at the painting

Did the snow appear cold
Were our feet red with it, with the wet snow

And then what were our names
Did you love me or did I misunderstand

      Is it terrible

Do you intend to come back

Do you hear the world's keening

Will you stay the night

Ever

Never, never, never, never, never.

—KING LEAR

Even now I can't grasp "nothing" or "never."
They're unholdable, unglobable, no map to nothing.
Never? Never ever again to see you?
An error, I aver. You're never nothing,
because nothing's not a thing.
I know death is absolute, forever,
the guillotine-gutting loss to which we never say goodbye.
But even as I think "forever" it goes "ever"
and "ever" and "ever." *Ever after.*
I'm a thing that keeps on thinking. So *I never see you*
is not a thing or think my mouth can ever. Aver:
You're not "nothing." But neither are you something.
Will I ever really *get* never?
You're gone. Nothing, never—ever.

Mistaken Self-Portrait as Persephone
in the Desert

One hot afternoon, I toured the old prison for POWs.

There are no people here, only facilities for holding them.

One doesn't think of the Underworld as being bright,

but I lived in the desert, under that big sky, as if I were belowground.

I watched a film of a Beckett play. *I love order,* Clov says at one point.
It's my dream.

A world where all would be silent and still, and each thing in its last place, under
the last dust.

In the desert there is order. All the prisoners were silent and still and in
their places.

And then you know what. The blisterfire bombs, shudder-thuds, flood-
lights, dazed
cracks, canines.

Of course, this chaos is their minds.

In reality they lie on cots the long, hot afternoons, and paint murals

of the land they see from their windows. It's this detail I find so—

imagine being in prison and drawing what lies just outside: humps of nothing,
     dun-yellow needles, flat vulture sky.

We must accept who we are.

Proust said, The real voyage of discovery consists not in seeking
     new landscapes, but
                              in having new eyes.

When I dream, I dream that my mother was never frightened for me.

In the painting at the house I stay in there is a film being shown,
     a celluloid film.

A child asks for more. Then she's leaving the orphanage,

a suitcase in her tiny hand, a box of food, a waiting train.

She is rubbing her eyes, trying to see, and my mother

is rubbing her back, warm hand on bone.

They're not thinking of the land they left behind, of all they've lost.

So I'm painting the desert before us. Look:

the dry scrub   the yellows and blues

the sharp eyes of cactus needles

Expecting

I'm six months along
and I wonder why nobody
told me. I've got red wine
in my right hand, a cigarette
in my left. There's
a noisy party all
around me. I put down
the glass and lift my shirt.
The baby's there, visible
under my transparent
skin, a little girl, wearing
bluebird barrettes.
I think she's mad at me.
What a lush!
she's thinking.
Her hair is gold,
too short for barrettes,
so I wonder if they're
actually part of her skull. She's
got blue veins all under
her skin. My stomach
wobbles like Jell-O.
*It's time for her to be
born,* another guest at the party
says, and my dead mother

helps me lift the pregnant belly off,
unscrewing it like a cork.
Little girl, I'm sorry
I took no prenatal
vitamins, I ate the sushi,
which was delicious,
and today the newspaper
led with a story
about impoverished zoos
deciding which species
they'll no longer
protect and breed. But there's
room for you. I just
didn't know what to think,
I just didn't know how to think of you.

Miscarriage

your romantic, imprecise side:
the time you glimpsed   a hawk on the road
and thought it was your mother—

a conception
misled by want

Mistaken Self-Portrait as Mother of an Unmade Daughter

Do you not want to be alive?
I can't say I don't understand—

To bring something into the world,
a creature that will be ruled by the conflict between its "will"
    and its impulses, surroundings, limitations. . . .

We choose many things, but we can't say we choose existence.
My existence is not *mine*
the way my opinions are, my blue crepe pants,
my taste for cherries.

My existence belongs in some sense to my parents, and to
the universe—or God, if you believe in god.

It belongs to evolution,
the galaxy and the space beyond,
to black holes, to red dwarfs, to
hydrogen and oxygen and carbon.

My existence belongs to iron.

I understand, in a way, my body's
reluctance

to impose existence on another—

      and yet I—   I almost feel you are real

and I know you, turning over the beach shell in my hands,
remembering the red sailboat shirt you wore all this summer,

with a button for the yellow sun—

.

With my small phone always tucked about my person

under the great lavender sky I'll set forth
on a pilgrimage

to the bridge that way   accept

the noble truth

which is to be absorbed
in the enormity of it without fail

even if the precipice
keeps leaving you voicemails—

•

Perhaps you don't come
because it's more painful
to me to have you
than not to?

: the person who first put a boat
in a bottle
and later wondered
why she'd had the impulse
to contain—

•

Before you have sight
the colors sway underneath your eyes
like kelp.

It is false to speak like this, but
false not to speak of you—

all the language I have for you
is ornamental—

but the sun is no ornament

go out and see it
stand under it rushing onward
let the body go borderless and drained

a scrim

for the light to come through.

At Père Lachaise

It wasn't always going to be like this.
You were going to read books and grow up
and understand more. You weren't going
to bury people, you were going to study
Proust's gray-black grave at Père Lachaise
and read the note the French girl left there.
Who was she with her bobbed hair, her violin case?
One day you would die but it was so far away
time itself would be different by then—
only time is not different as the years go by
just faster and it gets harder not easier to die.
So you practice: climb the blue and unremembered hills,
catch your breath on the bridge
between the cliffs, trumpet flowers
blooming like the robber barons' wild hair.
Your first bike was blue with ribbons,
you called her BlueBell.
Along Pierrepont Street you sped
wondering who Pierre was and where
his bridge had been: were you now
riding over it unable to see the chasm
of violet rocks below your pedaling feet—?
Proust you are dead but I am reading
your white bones your black words.
I laugh aloud in the French interior designer's

soft white bed eating a pistache macaron.
When we die gloved in earth we'll wonder why
we ever felt aswim in shame the lawns of June
were ablaze the lawns ablaze

Interlude (Posthumous)

When I'm dead

my daughters

will shuffle their impossible bodies
along the tombstone's soft grass,
and on the damp stone
lay their cheeks, saying

Mother, why did you not
value us?

II

What It Was Like

Your green mind is an ocean you can't enter,
sleeping in the bed hours each day.
Blurry figures move in the rooms around you.
Someone cooks a Christmas feast. Another buys
complicated, precise plastic goods,
distributes them around the house.
The past opens into a lamp, a bee colony,
a book about mitochondria under attack.
You want to be alone in the deep,
the spiky sea urchins drifting along the floor,
the fish starting and shivering, the reef fading.
Instead you're like the dead in deadpan.
In the subway the billboards ask
DID I REALLY DIE? The snow on the sidewalk
graying. The buckets of footsteps gone.
You keep saying, this is my hand,
it hurts, please take it away.
Hating and wanting in equal measure,
jealous of the others' human time,
the way their bodies work:
cells dividing, cytokines quiet.
Not yours. You stare at the ceiling,
eating superfoods, taking pills, rubbing
your liver with castor oil,
spooning down maca and nettles.

Notebook pages scrawled with the facts:
the what–went–wrong–and–how, the police
searchlight squall of pursuit, the verdict
always about to be delivered.

Idiopathic Illness

I threw hollowed self at your robust,
went for IV drips, mercury detoxes, cilantro smoothies.
I pressed my lips to you, fed you kale, spooned down coconut oil.
I fasted for blood sugar, underboomed the carbs,
chased ketosis, urine-stripped and slip-checked.
Baked raw cocoa & mint & masticated pig thyroids.
You were contemporary, toxic, I can't remember what you were,
you're in my brain, inflaming it, using up the glutathione.
I read about you on the Internet & my doctor agreed.
Just take more he urged *& more.*
You slipped into each cell. I went after you with a sinking inside
and medical mushrooms for maximum *oom*, I plumbed
you without getting to *nevermore*. O doom.
You were a disease without name, I was a body gone flame,
together, we twitched, and the acupuncturist said, it looks difficult,
stay calmish. What can be said? I came w/o a warranty.
Stripped of me—or me-ish-ness—
I was a will in a subpar body.
I waxed toward all that waned inside.

Human-Sized Pain

It was a *me* I couldn't let go,
in Sauconys and sweat-wicking shirts,
in mules and a miniskirt, in fear, in numbness,
virusy, wired and dumb, and all of a sudden
praying. I shuddered a little like
one does in a dream. The pain
arrived as if from inside me,
reaching out of my marrow into my mind.
I tried to act, to alleviate, to assuage.
But it didn't get better
with time; time made it worse.
To know my pain you had
to want what I wanted but not have it,
you had to watch the years unfurl
into yellow leaves without leaving.
No, forget the leaves—too poetic.
To know it you had to live without,
while those around you lightly *had*
and had and kept on having.
I believed less and less
in the future. All that possibility,
dwindled to a nothing, but.
Four, five, six, the months,
four, five, six, the years.
It was an image in a photograph

that kept getting blurrier
even as the resolution grew clearer.
It's not like missing the dead
or wanting another chance at love;
it shimmers on lakes,
is especially strong in the summer,
clinging to me like a person
who can't swim but wants
to be in the water, a thing
that will drown me
just to show me who I am.

Poem (Problem)

I kept trying to put the pain into a poem,
but all I did was write the word "pain"
in my notebook, over and over.

A Note on Process

1.

I began by keeping track of my time. It was February and the
snow had been falling all morning. I rarely saw any people on the
sidewalk outside, though I could detect the traces of their passage,
which the fresh snow quickly covered. I was reading a book about
a gymnast whose body seemed to contain an important mystery. I
read a little and then I watched archival footage on YouTube, so
I could see it "for myself." I surrounded myself with this moment.

2.

Watching the gymnast land a dismount from the uneven bars gave
me a sense of infinite possibility, as if the routine were a process
occurring over and over and over. I was a girl wanting to be a
gymnast, studying her photographs—her gravity-defying body—
in the small hot gym where I practiced. And I was thirty-seven
with a body that didn't work.

3.

The routine of my days was itself without shape or end, although
I understood there would be an ultimate end.

4.

When I finished her biography I made a list of what I had "done" all day. This was a failure, as it should have taken as much time to write as living itself did. But failing was fine with me. I wanted to formulate myself around a list written in precise ink, not merely to fall asleep on the couch again, to slip under.

5.

I went to the kitchen to take a drug the doctors had given me, a little imploring thing.

6.

What did I know about glory at that age? the gymnast wrote in her memoir. *To me, competing was about improving my body and mind—overcoming frustrations, anger, and jealousy so that, in one shining moment, my body became a tool driven by unwavering concentration and desire.*

7.

The clip of the gymnast doing her perfect routine never lost its patina for me. In it I could see the will honed to a fine tool, a ferocious act of attention. This was a process I couldn't imagine not being part of—

Even as I had begun to reconcile myself to exactly that.

Caged in a body that would not let me escape it—;

8.

The gym I used to practice in was stuffy, with two blue landing
mats, a whirring box fan, and an urn of chalk beside the uneven
bars. Girls in leotards and scrunchies clapping the excess powder
from their hands, giggles and the silence of effort.

At practice, I stretched and made myself small and still

doing a split on the red felt beam

pushing the stretch past comfort into pain

9.

       to be elegant,
          self-forgetful.

10.

I loved the clean container of my leotard, the bright spangles.

11.

A year earlier, something had gone awry in the minute biological particulars of my body. No one understood what it was. Trapped in a body that wasn't working right, I couldn't work, couldn't think. Time got sticky and meaningless. The fatigue so profound it swallowed me.

Everyone's tired, a friend said, from across the chasm, one day when I managed to get out of the house.

12.

The gymnast was very slim. Her hair was always in pigtails or ponytails, tied with thick bright yarn. Her body was taut from hours of practice. Yet in competition it appeared almost as if she had forgotten her will, had come to effortlessly inhabit her own grace.

13.

I had no fear, she wrote, *and I never said, "I cannot do that."*

14.

I was terrified that I couldn't get my mind to work. I was terrified of the pain, with the unpredictable electric shocks buzzing up and down my legs. I was terrified in the way I'd been when, as a child, I suddenly realized I was going to die. The rocks I gathered at the stream by the red barn country house suddenly weighing me down.

15.

In my diary I listed what I'd done in practice: thirty back walk-overs; ten valdezes; three handstands on bars, the double turns on beam, a half-on, half-off. *By the end of the year I know I will beat Marta on the beam.*

At practice the coaches told us to *stay tight* and *create a space under your arms* and to *stick it keep your legs tight.* We were always hollow and light, we were always spotting, choosing a place to look and looking for it alone.

16.

To want something so much that you become that thing. To defy the container of the body through the obsessive remaking of it.

17.

Maybe what I'm saying is that I wanted the possibility that the female body could become numinous.

18.

Through extreme self-use, through obsession
with the spiritual potential of obsession—

19.

My palms tore open from the friction on the uneven bars—a "rip." At lunch, a friend offered me a palm reading. The rip, she told me, had torn through my heart line. There goes love, she said, laughing.

The pain was clean and clear. The tear never fully healed.

20.

Mastering a skill is an invention of authority. But any invention is anti-authority. The writer Paul Valéry said once, "Two dangers never cease threatening the world: order and disorder."

21.

Once a week I took the bus for twenty-three minutes to get my
blood drawn. The room smelled of urine. The lab technicians put
on latex gloves, tapped my vein, and stuck a needle in. At first they
were diffident. Then we had an understanding. The kinder one
patted me on the shoulder, told me about her two-year-old. The
tougher case called me "Ms. O." She never said hello.

Once, though, she let me hear her complain about the other patients,
then said, "I use the smallest needle on you, because your veins are tiny."

22.

A subplot: I was trying to conceive a child, and I could not. It
took a long time before I understood why: my body had fallen
out of immunotolerance (the understanding that parts of the self,
organs, blood proteins, the like, are not to be attacked by the
body's own immune system).

Instead I lived in—well, we could call it immune-chaos. It was difficult
not to think metaphorically about this:

I was under attack from *myself,*
attacked by the very biology that was designed to keep me "safe"

23.

and the result was that I was not myself.

24.

There is no way to demarcate suffering. What one "feels" when "suffering" is not like a date in history but like a day that cannot be logged.

25.

The thrill when you try something difficult for the first time— reaching blindly for the bar as you jump backward over it. When I was sick, my head throbbed in the mornings, my limbs heavy as the ocean. The lymph nodes on my neck swelled to the size of mothballs.

26.

I spent half of most days on websites dedicated to the identification of "mysterious ailments." Mainly I read comments threads for hours. The chains of thought and argument were peculiar, even pathological—but also comfortingly predictable.

I wrote comments and didn't post them, but as I wrote my heart rate went up and my cheeks flushed, as if I were exercising or aroused.

27.

Keats, ill, said to his friend Charles Brown:

I have an habitual feeling of my real life having past, and that I am leading a posthumous existence.

Charles was going to go with him to Italy, but never did.

28.

There was one upside: mosquitoes no longer bit me.

I was me but in disguise.

29.

My muscles, my skin, got molded, my brain got firm.
My will got girled and fierce.
I took the bus home by myself
in my Adidas gym socks and shoes,
continuous and used up,

muscle by muscle,
tricep to adductor, oblique
by oblique, psoas to calf.
Having stuck the landing
my rips bleeding.

Everything was measurable, improvable.

30.

But improvement wasn't the only goal.

We had stickers on our hands and glitter on our shiny blue leotards
with white zigzags. Mastering a skill was a joy, an addiction, unhurried
and luxurious, a way out of yourself and a way in all at once. A girlness
fabricated and internalized, but shimmery and ribboned—useful, not
useful, it didn't matter.

It's play, which is its own process. The point is joy.

31.

I kept trying to apply the model of will to the sick body to rise off
the bed, like a phoenix. All I had were clichés.

32.

One day I went for a run determined *Just do it*. I told myself
Whatever doesn't kill you only makes you stronger. Gray clouds, an
ichor air. The pine needles browning. My legs shaking and numb,
my arms full of heavy sand. Home, I collapsed back into bed.

33.

The chalking up, the grips, the stretching, the Ace bandages, the
velvety feel of the floor mat, the bounce of the fiberglass bars,
their give underhand. Trying. Then doing it again.

The slightest loss of attention leads to death, the poet said.

34.

Then puberty.
The little plush pockets of fat on the inner thighs.
"Menstruation," irregular because of all the workouts.
Plum-black blood, stains on the perfect sheen of the leotards,
as if we soiled them just by becoming ourselves.

35.

All winter, I kept track of time from my blue couch, reading comments on the Internet, taking my pills, making lists with a fine black pen, watching videos of the gymnast. It made the panic slide away, put some light back in.

36.

(all I can say is the illness was like that state between sleep and wakefulness when you aren't sure where or who you are—

37.

"I" a ghost in the machine, a surreptitious invention, a robot mind, a white noise, a soul whaled in, a hoard.)

38.

Because I was told my sickness was exacerbated by stress, I played at being "normal"—cooking, resting, slowing down. The irony is, this retraction to a narrower set of possibilities was similar to the experience of my friends who were new mothers.

39.

Early on, you learn not to be scared bending backward unable to see
where you are going.

The process is control and letting go, surrender to whatever will happen.

Once you get used to reaching backward
you do back handsprings on a line on the basketball court, then the low
beam, the coach stacking mats next to it.
The body learning what your mind wants to do with it

One morning my hands miss the beam,
my wrist snaps back, tearing the tendon.

X-ray, splint, the doctor tells me I can't compete for six weeks.
I have a meet tomorrow, I say. My mother lets him tape it up.

Always that backward reach   trusting your body knows
more than your mind.

40.

It's when you think about it that things go wrong.

41.

My acupuncturist told me, "You think too much." I wasn't sure
how to stop. I practiced blankness for a while, read the newspaper.

42.

Another definition of process is "a series of actions or steps taken
in order to achieve a particular end." But I thought there might
be no end, except the end I didn't want.

43.

Before summer camp, boys, or calculus, before stonewashed
denim, before we threw away the Keds, the Benetton shirts, the
friendship bracelets, before college. Long before we threw away
the leotards with their fine stitching, shiny bodices—

44.

What begins as a kind of ordered disorder (trying to fly) becomes
a disordered order (trying to control your body, keep it a child's).

45.

"One is not born, but rather becomes, a woman," wrote Simone de
Beauvoir.

46.

It is not coincidental that the gymnast later got breast augmenta-
tion and became a spokesperson for Botox.

47.

One day I went to a new doctor. He asked me if I wanted chil-
dren, and said, "Time is not on your side."

48.

When I was twelve, I wore a blue windbreaker every day, even in
ninety-degree heat. I didn't want my changing body to be seen.
By August, the windbreaker was filthy, with streaks of dirt on its
sleeves, the cuffs turned gray. Take it off, my mother always said.
Take off your coat and stay a while. But I didn't want to stay—I
wanted to go back.

49.

The terror of adolescence is the terror of being seen; in this case,
seen as *female*, your thoughts made as comical and disgusting as
your habit of bleeding.

50.

At thirteen I thought I could hide my body under clothes. Then
I thought I could hunger it into androgyny. I could be a self that
was not exactly girl.

But I also wanted to be as girlish as the gymnasts I loved—all glitter,
no earth, gaps between their thighs.

51.

Even as I got better and stronger on the balance beam, I felt more
uncertain. Did what I look like match who I was?

I tried to remember the joy I used to feel.

52.

The sick body is always having speech seized from it. One day, when I pleaded for help, the doctor frowned.

You don't have a bad disease, she said.

When I told her, *I think something else is going on,* she took the speech and hid it away. Even as I say this, I worry my words appear to be without grounds.

53.

Always at the back of my mind: I had tried, but had I tried hard enough?

54.

There are many scripts for proceeding but of course you want the one that is denied to you, a friend told me.

55.

I mean the possibility of grace, which is something.

56.

I object to certain kinds of masochism, the way that some women
like to glamorize their sexual neediness.

But maybe I just like the part of female pain (or bravery) that insists on
its privacy. This may be a failing in me.

57.

There is a video of me speaking in public at this time, a low pilot
flame of myself. After the event, I told someone I was not sure I
wanted to continue to live.

58.

Then in the snow one day something happened.
It—a part of me—broke inside my body.

At the hospital they said I had internal bleeding, problems they could find.
After blood tests, probes, and EKGs

they prescribed me medicine, rest, treatments

—and I began to return from the gray world of stinging skin and sand-heavy limbs—

59.

When I tell the story I speak of this nadir and of the eventual turn.
But it would be wrong to pin the drama of transformation on one night—

60.

I thought of what the gymnast said. "To me, competing was about the next time and the one after that. It was about improving my body and mind."

61.

Alice James, Henry and William's sister, was unwell all her life, and diagnosed by doctors with hysteria. In her forties she learned she had breast cancer and would soon die. "To him who waits, all things come!" she exulted to her diary. For years, she had "longed and longed for some palpable disease." Until now her illness had been a "monstrous mass of subjective sensations" she felt "personally responsible for."

She died months later.

62.

What if—and this was the question I couldn't bear—
the rest of my life was just this:

the process of surviving?

When in fact *I* had not survived.

63.

I was the mouthpiece for the illness, I could translate it, but even I
was not sure what it was saying.

64.

My handwriting in the log got smaller and smaller.

More and more went unrecorded.
But I will not speak of that.

65.

(When I got sick, I did think, if I die now, I have spent way too
much time listening to men talk.)

66.

There is nothing sustaining about sickness

and because there is no end, there can be no "goal"
and because there is no goal there is

no process
                    : so what is there?

67.

Of course you could say all life is exactly like this.
"I shall soon be quite dead at last in spite of all," Beckett wrote.

But I think the good life is more like gymnastics—

a futile grace.

68.

After all this time, I am not sure how to describe the gymnast's mystery. But for a moment that night under the white-black sky I understood:

69.

the distinct moment when the snow coats the streets
enough that our passage can be seen through it
tracings of pure being—

a will that could burn you, filling a form she made with her own mind—

70.

I wanted to believe the process of watching the days go by was enough. Even in a body whose processes were corrupted,

71.

through long months when death, the body's failure, waited down the block.

But.

72.

Imagine a line like the one at the gym on which you practice
just for the sake of trying,
for the value of it, which is its own joy.
Landing. Sticking it.
Not because the judge is waiting in the corner
for your final salute. But just because.
To land it. To do it over and over, to feel it.
It's like a hunt for light in the body.

The line is uncorrupted even if the body might be.
No, I don't like that old-fashioned, purist way of thinking.
How about: the body is
exhausted but the line is not,
and look glitter on the floor
and the leg a little ribbon shine!

III

Some Aspects of Red and Black in Particular

One of the destructive assumptions of our time is that ideas have
no originators.
—DONALD JUDD

I know large forces move us
like tides, and yet in the salt flats
of this desert I sometimes think I see
a horseman riding through the scrub
at first a speck, then a small dot, a growing
dark blotch sorting itself
into hat, head, horse, mind—

Mistaken Self-Portrait as Demeter in Paris

You can only miss someone when they are still present to you.

The Isle of the Dead is both dark and light.

Henry Miller told Anaïs Nin that the real death is being dead while
  alive.

The absent will only be absent when they are forgotten.

Until then, absence is a lie, or an oxymoron.

Sometimes I want to be famous once more, and then I think about the
  paparazzi. . . .

I value my solitude. But I fear I am dead while alive.

To avoid living, worry about all you've forgotten.

When I miss my daughter, it's as a kind of idea. Then she comes to me:
  in her corduroy red parka, hair sticking out,
  smiling at the geese, eating her shoelaces,
  pointing, crying, More!

When I saw the movie, in the dark center of winter, I thought:

The son wasn't trying to say goodbye to his dying father. He was trying to say
  forever.

Alone so much, I think about the people whose stories I learn in
   books.

The lover of Picasso who didn't understand why her grandmother

went so often to the graves of her children and husband.

Just wait, her grandmother said. You will see.

No, what she said is, There comes a time when, past your moment,

you live for external things: a slice of sky through your window,

a painting you'll see only three more times   a painting

where the colors are everything.

Poem of Regret for an Old Friend

What you did wasn't so bad.
You stood in a small room, waiting for the sun.
At least you told yourself that.
I know it was small,
but there was something, a kind of pulped lemon,
at the low edge of the sky.

No, you're right, it was terrible.
Terrible to live without love
in small rooms with vinyl blinds
listening to music secretly,
the secret music of one's head
which can't be shared.

A dream is the only way to breathe.
But you must
find a more useful way to live.
I suppose you're right
this was a failure: to stand there
so still, waiting for—what?

When I think about this life,
the life you led, I think of England,
of secret gardens that never open,
and novels sliding off the bed

at night where the small handkerchief
of darkness settles over
one's face.

Mistaken Self-Portrait as Meriwether Lewis

In the spring of 1804 Meriwether Lewis and William Clark left their camp near St. Louis, Missouri, to map the unknown West. Lewis was known for "depressions of the mind."

Strange morning. I woke without remembering
who I was. A minute passed. Blue glass beads
hung on a string beside me in the tent.
I lay under a buffalo robe covered with ink sketches
resembling the path of a crow on wet sand.
I knew what a "buffalo robe" was.
I did not know who I was.
The wind, which almost moaned, I knew—it reminded me of something:
myself? Then emptiness, the gut-drop
into the abyss of the self, the most silent fall
of a stone before it hits the water:
My name is Lewis.

•

The doctor told me faults run through us all,
that scars extend far beneath the skin, cruder
in repair, but stronger, too. He has always tried
to make me feel my sickness as a strength.
Sometimes it does seem to me there is water
in those faults, that if scars
catch the light at the right angle
they pull the sun within—

something wants to pull me.
Something must want to pull me. I feel it pulling
and widen like want:

a day, a day of daylight,
instead of this dogged night.

.

Tall as a fir tree, slippery and hard to hold
as a far fish in a near lake, ablaze with resentment,
a corpse that will not forfeit dream,
a corpse that lives like a lantern.
And goes on, like that, for a long time.

.

Today I am my own shadow—
the sun is always overhead.

.

A hard week with the men.
Yesterday's road was excessively dangerous—
along this creek a rocky path,

so steep that if man or horse were precipitated from it
they would be dashed to pieces.
The men were nervous, high-strung.
Then Frazier's horse fell from the road
& rolled with his load near a hundred yards
into the Creek—. We expected
the horse was killed

                         but to our astonishment

when the load was taken off
he arose to his feet & appeared to be but little
injured   Galloping along the grass
which blazed beneath!

Were my own path so
green, were I to know it so—

.

When you are mapping
                         the future

you see a path to what?

—to water, a kind of resignation
to the inevitable; an old man
who is thinner than you, with frail
bones, has heard more music, never
stopped loving the inevitable
rush of nights with spirits and whiskey's
self-undoing—

to have an acute need is to be hungry;
to have an illness that never makes itself known
nor absent is to be
in a constant noon, the almost dead of day.

.

I am not Meriwether Lewis, I think.
I wake to a body that hangs on me
like bad tailoring.
The seconds arrive as if in delay—
it is nature to forget we are nature,
the aching-toward-extinction of flesh.
I have never seen such animals as this gray squirrel,
ratty but voracious, rooting
at the beech's base today. The body
I read to at night is voracious, it wants light

to blind it; breathe, I say to myself
Meriwether Lewis. The candle burns.
I hear it being consumed. It keeps
the little animals away.

                    —But how strange
that it is not my eyes that make the world!
To be consumed or else to be nothing!

•

I am Lewis, I know, but I forget myself. . . .
Our diet is very meager, whale oil and biscuits.
The crane I shot fed only
three of us, but was divided twelve ways;

a flaw within widens

a cacophony a concatenation
a catastrophe;

Do they think they are natural men, my comrades?

•

To make a map of this country
is to make and mark the wounds—

it is strange to be the oppressor
when you don't even know it—

his knife is my knife, his mouth mine,

but here in the wild all I mean to do is
look, measure, take stock—

·

Before I left I walked into the woods
near our settlement
and saw him on his horse—
he wouldn't let me
take
        what I needed, what needed to be taken—

I sense it near, the meaningful end.
But the men turn back, the dog Seaman
has died; on we go to the end where the water
rushes over the edge
and into the borderless pool
widening and widening—

.

A sickness that got into the water,
—it made the others ill
and now the spring we camp beside
    is suspect. Later they will ask me if I think
ignorance is an excuse—
I am a past tense that is
always present,
                I must walk on
to where the borders will be
the scars that tendril
beneath the land.
I walk the sickness with me,
dragging my viral cape
across the earth and through its waters.
    —I am glorious,
and wrong.

Unnatural Essay

1.

For many years I lived a normal life. Normal to some. Hotel Privilege. Etc., etc., as they say.

But when I became sick,

I discovered what I had always naturally called *I* was really no longer an "I."

It changed all the time—in fact, entirely receded as a coherent notion—according to something happening in my cells that no one could identify.

I felt dispersed, lacking a center, my eyes plastic.

Walking, teaching, writing, I experienced myself as categorically fraudulent. (Or should I say "I" felt categorically fraudulent.)

I had a face but it was like a mask. Language torqued, unusually murky. This was not an observation about semiotics, the gap between word and thing. Now I was living in the gap.

In the past, I had quoted Emerson: "Our moods do not believe in each other."

"I" had also quoted, with theoretical admiration, Rimbaud's "je est un autre."

I saw how wrong I was: the very fact that I'd been able to think this way suggested an unappreciated coherence.

Now, "I" was tired. Almost unable to walk down the block. My body was melting, distorted, like a Gaudí, or a—I can't remember his name. Fatigue so extreme, I no longer had any real desires.

It took a long time, strangely, to realize this was not normal.

Once I did I sought help.

But because no one, not even the doctors in white coats, could identify the source of the problem, "I" wondered if it was all in "my" head.

Then one day, after months, the lab work showed something a little "funny."

Aha! I thought. I'm *not* myself. Like a computer

infected by Internet malware.

2.

A capture of a capture,
a name not sweet.
Running commentary in my
pain-disturbed sleep: "Thou art thyself."
"What's Montague? it is nor hand, nor foot,
Nor arm, nor face, nor any other part
Belonging to a man."
So maybe just:
Be some other name—not
sick. Not pain.

3.

Some days I did well—the mask fell away, I tried to pinpoint what
had allowed me to recover my *I*-ness, even as I was buried in subreddit
threads and Yahoo groups about ATP processes, mitochondrial diseases,
neuropathy, MTHFR mutations.

4.

A woman in a white coat with a small dachshund under her desk told
me my immune system was malfunctioning.

"Antibodies to cell DNA."
I had "sticky blood" because my body was attacking its proteins.
I was not absorbing iron.
My metabolic processes were not functioning correctly.
I was failing to "clear" viruses.

And so I became absorbed in the medical details.

The body began to seem an inevitably fragile, miraculous organism,
full of mutations and bacteria and viruses and poor DNA repair.

It was just an accumulation of trillions of cells making mistakes all the time—
and one day it would make too many mistakes.
One day it already had—

a plane's contrails unzipping the sky.

5.

Kept thinking about how to put it:
Dead, but sleeping underneath.
Hence, some return possible. Some capture

of the past in the morrow.
Honeysuckle at the bus stop. Sudden hope.

("O, that you were yourself!"—another self, a future self, a natural self; any self; self-possessed. Whispered to that none-self, that nonesuch: you had a mother,

let your daughter say so.)

6.

But I looked well, thanks to all the supplements, the raw pig glands, the N-acetylcysteine and sunshine bathing, the nerve blocks and the raw coconut oil, the glandulars, the shots of Nrf2 energizers, the mitochondria cocktails, adjuvant therapies.

7.

Now that I was sick, I looked back and saw that before—even when I thought I was healthy—I was already not.

For years, my energy had suddenly faded, a candle flickering out, a computer freezing.

Let's put it this way: My sickness in some sense is natural to me.

So what is the natural old me I yearn for?

Reading late into the humid July night; jogging in the fog. Lying on the sloping floor and watching *Star Trek* reruns; conversations poured out of ourselves.

8.

Natural / unnatural: even if my sickness were natural it had clearly reached an *unnatural* point, a point at which "I" denatured.

9.

There *had* been an I
that had its boundaries—
there *is* a natural

from which we can be utterly estranged.

10.

Would a rose by another name smell so sweet?

I couldn't remember.

11.

Sickness made me a good girl who couldn't leave my house.

I snuck cigarettes under the roof's eaves and hissed at the squirrels.

I dumped the green juice down the sink.

12.

A rose is a rose is sore is a rose is an or

13.

(During this time I had a dream I went to a desert where words were aflame and I was a very bad artist, hectic and febrile, unsure exactly what my desert looked like, because I kept looking at my own burning hands rather than the landscape around me. Flat sky, vulture eyes, prickly pear cacti, silt from China, spiders, scorpions, a fine white sand, rare cloud, involuted like a brain. I enjoyed being this artist.

I grew ecstatic at an hour of lead that became days of gold.

Death is metal used up, an element gone, the star collapsing: extended contemplation of it.)

14.

When, once before, I had a yearning I could not put in words, it was my slowly diminishing body (the clavicles and hip bones and back ribs) that articulated the pain (I thought). Although it did not. It said nothing other than underfed.

But I thought it expressed everything that language failed to express. A nonesuch self. Sweet and honorable and pure husbandry.

I was a misinterpreter of selfhood.

15.

When I got sick, I thought my body was speaking my own mess and that it was my problem to deal with.

For some time I thought I could survive by disciplining my mind and body.

As I suffered, I thought, obscurely, it was my fault—
as sometimes it was, due to wine, and chocolate, and cocaine or sex.

I half-believed my sick body was a failed language, a private thrift gone wrong.

I was failing, and my body was showing me so.

16.

In the end, such a simple answer!
A bacteria had invaded me, a prokaryote. It was a tiny organism that
had evolved to be able to penetrate tissue, shape shift, and hide.

But this answer was a story without an ending, a new problem. A conclusion
I couldn't deny but couldn't live with: My I was purely biological.

My words were
a poorly structured building.
The soil where my roses grow is pH 6.0 to pH 7.0, or else no roses.
The honeysuckle blooms only in May.

17.

I wanted to write an essay for you, a cold, cool essay.

I wanted its facets to cut. To be a capture: your own self in it, self-
shriven, ridden, forgiven.

I wanted to build an irrational castle of angles that made no sense—the
kind that would drive one mad, eventually. One that had angels in it.
Angels of desolation and gleaming torsos. They are the wind.

Instead I succumbed slowly to what I thought I'd walked away from.

18.

Was I merely flesh or something more?

19.

Or maybe I was making a mistake—I was still "I,"
but I was no longer the "I that was like such and such."

20.

Wanting the chance of a return, I bargain with god, with God, with
karma—

I put up the white sails.

But is it true?

Aren't I lying, when for once I should *really* tell the truth?
You can't bargain falsely with the gods: the whole force of the
bargain is your sincerity.

Oh no, the black sail.

21.

There was a line over which you could cross,
a line close to death,

> a line that took you out of the glimmering world
> so you flickered with the stench of death:

I had crossed from *I* into *this* and back to "I,"

and having crossed, went amiss—

the black sail always flickering

at the corner of my sight.

22.

I wish I could convey to you the urgency of this problem,

now that I am a letter that holds together again.

It is the thing I most want to do, and the thing I most cannot do.

The bus braking on the corner. A red traffic light. Coffee on an empty
stomach.

All these things so present.

Nothing was present: there was cotton wool between me and the world.

I felt no desire, nothing, really, except fatigue.

I had a glimmer of what it used to be like—but I also had adapted to circumstance.

I examine each line on my face.

This attempt is a necessary failure. You cannot use the brain to explain what happens when the mind's integrity fails, leaving biology in its place.

Fragile, sick, frail.

My mind no longer useful, therefore not virtuous.

Navesink

Before he died, blind and emaciated,
my grandfather, who loved the opera,
told me sometimes
among the tall trees he walked and
listened to the sound
of a river entering the sea
by letting itself be swallowed.

The Body in the Age of Mechanical Reproduction

> When neurons fire they make you feel something is happening, but it's
> nothing other than tissue creating an illusion of experience.
> —TED HONDERICH, "WHAT IT IS TO BE CONSCIOUS"

Returning from the procedure
      I sit in traffic sweating

made of tissue and cells but

I am thinking of the operating room
      doctor putting you within, and the green
around me deepens into three shades of green,

      a green joy

It didn't have to be
it could have felt like nothing
      made
            of nothing

2.

Before the procedure,
      I took a selfie in the
      waiting room

alone for the last hour
      (I hoped)

before my cells and its
articulately fused
an ugly room
      sailboat painting,
      curling magazines

On my screen I looked
so saturated,
      fingers on the phone
where I keep all the shots
      of myself to know
I am here (am I here)

The nurse was young, with a nose ring,
      she said my name intimately

I startled at
      her mouth.

3.

Days of Gonal-F and Lupron,
      ten 28 gauge
needles in the belly
pre-mixed agonist

ringing the navel
progesterone, 1.5 inches

(the medicine in your fat
dissolving stings
          more than the needle)

a half liter (by IV) of
immunoglobulins
          from thirty strangers

(pain from the Latin *poena* or
          penalty, and the Old French *peine*
or suffering, as punishment),

thirty people's defenses
against bacteria and viruses
spreading lake-cold up
the bicep's vein,

                    a glaze
of borrowed immunity—

(follow me little cell,
I'll make a home for thee)

So hush my body,
        stop attacking
all my little would-bes, stop

mistaking them   for harm

4.

Green things are furling and steepling,
they are in their spring,
                        the doctor
pathologizing the soil in shadow
        the slippery cavernous potential, the luteal sun,
corpses of leaves
        helixing—

a violent opening
at the movie theater unbuttoning
my jeans fat with drugs

and popcorn—

5.

Four days later a prick a cramp
the zygote attaches
two drops of blood bloom
and   they bloom

6.

We laid hand in   we lay in hand
I made room some room   we laid down the coil
and glass they laid the cells in   they
laid plans they in that room   I laid my
body on the steel   gurney I laid
me down to sleep   I laid anesthetic
the language   waylaid we   laid on the quiet
we laid our credit card on the   hush
little now I lay you   down we laid the green
card   on the receptionist's desk   laid
the green down   sticky on the cab's seat
we laid   we in the day we in the sun we

Mortals

In my mind I made you failproof: I pictured

the crib, the delicate hair, even the babysweet breath—
    I counted what I knew of the body, and copied it out

    diligently.

As they grunted and levered you
from the space I'd made
under my ribs
I saw I was the room
you had to leave to be yourself.

Emptily reaching out to hold you—

Poem for My Son

You were of the earth, like a lentil.
The taste of quince, a revulsion at meat.
The others were like a dream that scores
the body long after waking—
But you were sour spit, a pinched pain in the right hip.
There was nothing luminous about you,
oh you made the smells of the city repellent.
On the doctor's screen,
a black dot with a line through it, a blot,
you grew slowly gray and white,
then boned and legged and oblong and minded.
I made you out of grapefruit and Rice Chex.
—The others were made of longing.—
Each time I saw you in the sound waves
was preparatory, not romantic; not like the wind
but more like a river pushing against my legs,
insisting on its presence. In thick socks
I ate potato chips and congee, built
you without trying, splaying my rib cage.
Lugging my freight down the street,
I thought about what I wanted for you—
(love love and more love)
but you were already you, not
an outgrowth of my mind,

your own strange, remote, hardening body,
moving toward arrival under surgical lights
in sudden, open parenthesis—

The Window at Arles

Even the moon set him going, with its blank stare;
even the walls of the café, which seemed to tilt
and sway as he watched them, green with absinthe.
"It is a wonderful thing to draw a human being."
All night, van Gogh painted, and then scraped paint from his easel;
the stiff sound of palette knife on canvas,
scratching, made him think of a hungry animal.
Women came and posed.
"It is a wonderful thing to paint a human being, something
that lives," he told Theo. "It is confoundedly difficult,
but after all it is splendid."
When the money for models ran out,
he bought plaster casts of hands and hung them
from the room's crossbeams,
and woke to the sound of their knocking in the wind.

•

One night van Gogh sat in a chair, staring.
Brush in one hand, milk saucer in the other.
The tea was weak. Nothing came. In the morning,
one of his models brought bread and cheese
and made him eat. That afternoon,
he broke the plaster casts, banging hand against hand,
until in a storm of dust he stood coughing.

•

When he worked he felt a scratch at his calf,
a scarlet wound, a whoop of blood. He was hungry;
even his eyes were hungry.
All he saw was red: red snow, red legs of women
in the village *rues*, red pinwheels of hay.
"It is a wonderful thing
to hurt a human being, something
that lives. It is confoundedly difficult, but after all it is splendid."

Beyond the shadow, a cave opened
in the trees and led to emptiness,
a yellow you couldn't quite see an end to.
Van Gogh walked into it,
and his body began to shake. It was a color riot.
He could hear, somewhere, a dog
in the dark thumping its tail.
"How splendid yellow is!" he said.

•

Color is electricity, it turns you blind
if you get hold of it.
It turns you blind if something cold

gets hold of you and blisters.
Walls falling toward you.
When you turn color into a weapon,
something gets left
over: a charred body.
What you must do is take the plaster
and turn it to praise
as light turns the evening grass
to fear gone blind in the hunt.

How to Be

Like someone on a walk by the sea
thinking of bees and lavender,
like someone who stumbles and for a moment forgets the word "bees,"
looks up to find that the steel-blue sea has disappeared,
that his eyes blur with the snow static of an old TV —

(my life is a series of moments of persuading myself I'm free)

like a person whose language has
slipped away,
                        you stand on a promontory

with the snow general around you,

one foot in this world and one foot in the possible,
the ground we never think of as a surface,
the water into which we so easily fall,

and what if we do—?

ACKNOWLEDGMENTS

Thanks to the editors of the following anthologies, journals, and websites, in which versions of these poems originally appeared:

Academy of American Poets: "Mistaken Self-Portrait as Demeter in Paris" (as "Demeter in Paris"), "Ever"

Best of Best American Poetry (edited by Robert Pinsky): "The Window at Arles"

Best American Poetry 2008 (edited by Charles Wright): "The Window at Arles"

The Grey: "Mistaken Self-Portrait as Persephone in the Desert" (as "Persephone in the Desert")

Gulf Coast: "The Window at Arles"

The Kenyon Review: "Dread," "Self-Portrait as Myself," "Mistaken Self-Portrait as Mother of an Unmade Daughter," "Unnatural Essay"

The New Yorker: "Unforced Error"; "Poem of Regret for an Old Friend," "Navesink"

Poetry: "Sun In Days," "The Night Where You No Longer Live"

Ploughshares: "A Note on Process"

Plume: "Mnemonic"; "Addict Galerie"

Tin House: "Expecting" (as "Nightdream")

Virginia Quarterly Review: "At Père Lachaise"

I'm grateful to Cathy Park Hong, Monica Youn, Deborah Landau, David Baker, Eleanor Chai, Charles Simic, Paul Muldoon, Christian Wiman, and Katie Kitamura for their comments on early versions of these poems. Special thanks to the MacDowell Colony, the Corporation of Yaddo, the Guggenheim Foundation, and the Radcliffe Institute for Advanced Study at Harvard University for providing the time and mental space in which to write some of these poems. My deep thanks to my editor, Jill Bialosky, for her insights and comments, and to my agent, Chris Calhoun, for his support. And thanks to Jim, my first and best reader.

NOTES

"Addict Galerie": The title is taken from the name of a gallery in Paris.

"A Note on Process": The italicized quotations are drawn from Nadia Comaneci's Letters to a Young Gymnast and John Keats's letters.

"Some Aspects of Red and Black in Particular": The title of this poem is adapted from Donald Judd's essay "Some Aspects of Color in General and Red and Black in Particular"; the epigraph is taken from this essay, too.

"Mistaken Self-Portrait as Meriwether Lewis": The section concerning "Frazier's horse" is adapted from Lewis's journal.

"The Window at Arles": "It is a wonderful thing to paint a human being, something that lives. It is confoundedly difficult, but after all it is splendid." These lines are taken from Vincent van Gogh's letters to his brother Theo. Elsewhere in the poem, I modify the line for my own purposes.

"How to Be" owes a debt to Alice Oswald.